DARK EDITION

Variety Mandala

COLORING BOOK

A Coloring Book for Adults

VOL.3

Inspired Flowers, Animals, and Mandala Patterns

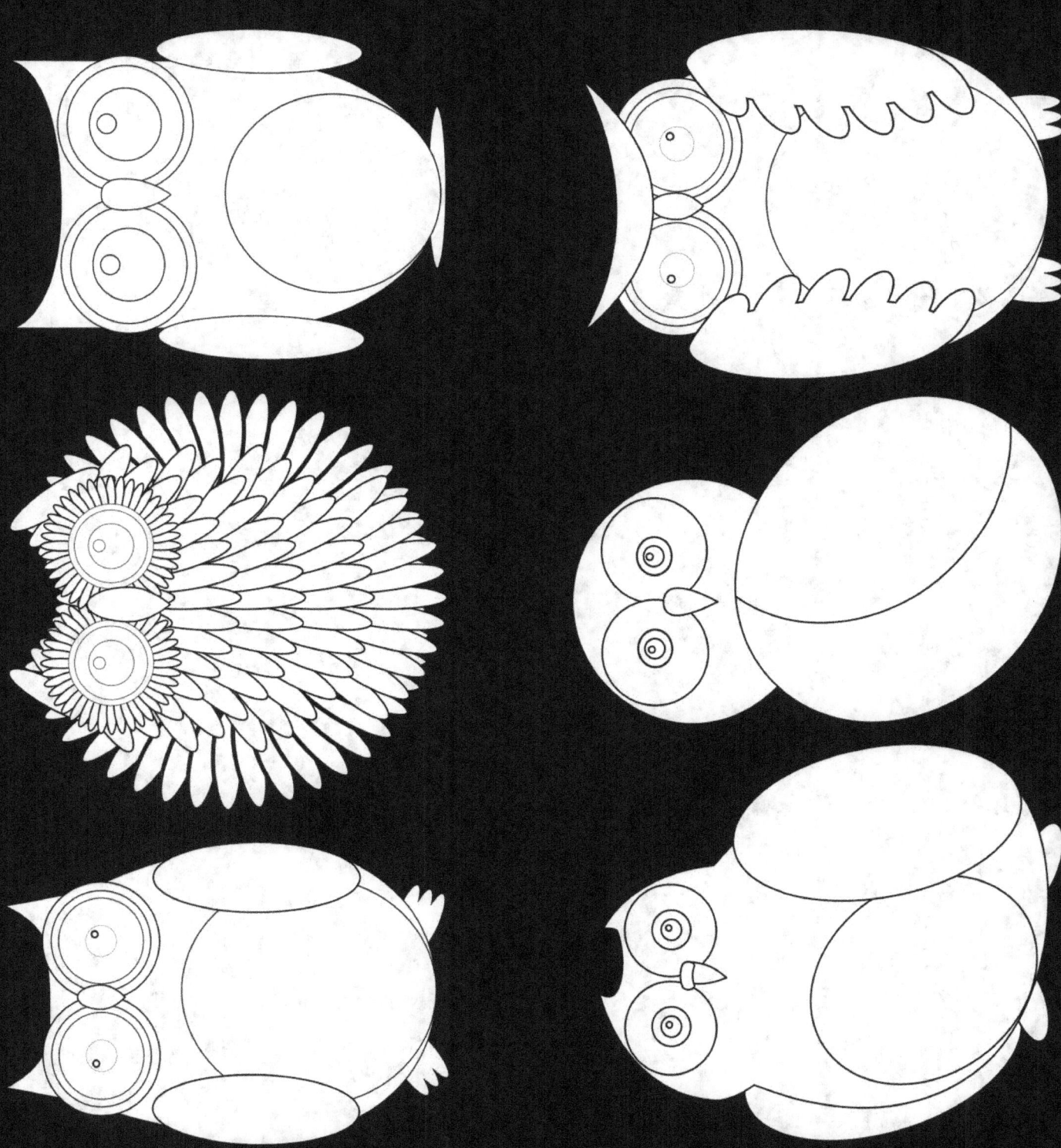

www.ingramcontent.com/pod-product-compliance
Lightning Source LLC
Chambersburg PA
CBHW081854280526
45789CB00007B/2695